Prison Segmentation For Miracles!

Rev. Mike Wanner

Table Of Contents

Introduction

Miracles are not as hard to find as many people think because you can pre-pave the path to the manifestation and the acceptance. As You Invite the Miracle, You plant A Seed that can attract Divine Energy and Human Support.

Typically, the word miracle that we are familiar with is not able to be explained in scientific terms. The occurrence of a miracle may not be evident from the natural order of things either.

The manifestation of the miracle may be attributed to God, a supernatural being, a deity, an angel, a miracle worker, a Saint, or religious leaders.

Informal language may describe an outcome that is unlikely from existing circumstances and events. A survivor walking away from a terrible auto wreck may be seen as a miracle manifested.

A person with a terminal illness can be viewed as having a miracle when the diagnosis is upgraded without a logical cause. The arrival of an infant itself can be seen as the miracle of birth.

The kind of miracles or Breakthrough that we will discuss now are the ones with spiritual preparation. If you really would like one, consider getting ready and staying ready.

As you shift to constant readiness, there becomes a kind of attraction field that envelops everything and everybody.

1 - Segmentation To Prepare For A Miracle

I have already introduced Segmentation in previous books and will just reference it here. Segmentation can reshuffle the space utilization and put fewer people in more spaces around the clock.

The primary goal is to spread people out and allow a more relaxed and less threatening environment. Coincidentally the process can increase safety and security by reducing occupancy in many places so when things happen anywhere; fewer people are in the area involved.

Facilities can create a B shift and a C Shift that will offer great new freedom possibilities for prisoners. Being able to select patterns or tracks of further segmentation that carries opportunities will promote feelings of personal empowerment and peace.

Management that chooses to make some adjustments based on this idea could have stress reduction throughout, and prisoners who are at higher risk may be more readily separated from potential conflicts with others.

Depression, fear, and helplessness do not contribute to the likelihood of miracles. Mental decisiveness and analysis and preparation can.

I have met so many people during my life that are looking for answers and benefits without making the choices necessary to find the clarity and prepare a reception space for the blessing to be grounded.

I like many others have lived through cycles of my life and questioned many things along the way and sought the answers to the question "What is right for me?"

As one grows up and follows a pattern, one may sometimes assume that the answers that we want are already preplanned. That may well be true, but please remember the phrase- "The Devil Is in the Details!"

Since we live in the physical world, we may wish all our answers to be available here for us. Inviting the energy needed to get the answers you seek from all dimensions or realms may be helpful.

You may align yourself with the information or energy of the miracles that you might like so that you may be able to find those possibilities. When you can see the image of the desired outcome, there can be a harmonic balance alignment with the goal that simplifies the manifestation by harmonious balancing out from you to the universe in a feedback loop, Like a Boomerang.

2 - Relaxed Hyperconsciousness & Miracles

Once upon a time, there were Magic Eye charts. Magic Eye Charts or posters to the casual observer look like a three-dimensional pattern.

Hidden within the pattern is/was a different pattern or image. The charts or posters came with instructions on how to develop towards a shift that can take your from a two-dimensional awareness to a three or more dimension awareness.

Now, this may sound very easy to do, but there are dynamics to the human psyche that may make the minds of many have a contra-productive uninvited reaction that can complicate the effort and frustrate the one trying. I became quite expert at being disappointed with this complication, and I do not recommend it.

Eventually, the lesson about the importance of relaxation emerged. If you get frustrated and try harder, it is less likely that you will be able to succeed.

My interpretation of the answer is that the effort that succeeds is when one is trying and attentive but somewhat relaxed or detached about achieving. The level of intensity needs to be diminished, so it does not give you stress.

Your control is vital so you can attract the Miracles that are subtly inside the picture you can easily see, like patterns in a Magic Eye Chart.

A psychologically initiated relaxation is the key to engaging dimensional shifting. I suggest that you do not struggle but breathe deeply and release and relax.

Please be aware that these words are from one who is not adept but continues to learn and grow in many areas of the human-divine interactive effort. The human-divine struggle of "in the world but not of it."

For your additional information, I have whole websites devoted to prayer and stress release which can help when you can access the internet. The sites are http://StressReleaseCoach.com and http://Create-A-Prayer.com.

3 - Prepare For A Miracle

How to prepare for a miracle? Notice I did not say "How to ASK for a miracle?" Asking God for a miracle may lead to a lack of faith if our prayer is not answered with the preciseness and speed of an Amazon order.

Our faith should not need a regular supply of miracles to survive. If you get lazy and do not want to do the work to prepare for your miracle, you could lose out and settle for less than God wants you to have.

If you have faith that a miracle worker will always make miracles come according to the worker's will, it could be a self-set trap. You may find yourself disappointed. Remember that "God helps those who help themselves (anon.)"

I suggest that you – Pray for the Miracle, Prepare for the Miracle, Release all attachment to the outcome, Embrace your patience, and Release all judgment. Go within and see what you might hear and be ready to follow instructions that might make little sense.

A request may be intensified when we ask God and also participate in the energy of expectancy and belief in unity with God. I invite your awareness to the idea whether you can recognize or feel the energy at any level.

Energy is said to follow thought, and I for one do believe it. Preparing is Ok and so is asking, but pivotal also is your involvement and expectations and action, so you do not miss it.

9

A
Course
In
Miracles

Publisher The Foundation For Inner Peace

Scribe: Dr. Helen Schucman

The Combined Volume, Third Edition of A Course in Miracles is the only edition that contains in one place all of the writings that, its Scribe, authorized to be printed. It is published solely by the Foundation for Inner Peace, the organization chosen by Dr. Schucman in 1975 for this purpose.

The Combined Volume also includes the Supplements to A Course in Miracles: "Psychotherapy: Purpose, Process and Practice" and "Song of Prayer." These sections are extensions of the Course principles, which were dictated to Dr. Schucman shortly after she completed A Course in Miracles.

5 - The Illusions That Humans Can See

Humans can have a very simplistic view of reality as they perceive it. Their individual interpretations of all that is viewed can be influenced by their earlier experiences; information shared with them, their descriptions of all that, and physical, emotional, mental, and spiritual energies that they felt in many configurations that they have blended consciously or subconsciously with all of that.

Life is not usually as simple as it may seem and one off target interpretation may influence and or trigger other variations and derivative variations that flow forth from that illusion.

The Course mentioned above is a map of sorts for following a perspective of all experiences in a way that allows the viewer to frame everything as authentically as possible. Taking a second look at things through a more transparent lens can give the ability to reassess any conclusions which were formed improperly because of false illusions.

A simple way to begin the process of investigating your interpretations is to get a version of the course as near to the challenges that you may wish to target.

Caution is recommended to select original information that is authenticated carefully. Misinterpretation on top of your unique interpretations could serve you less than optimally.

Many books and this one set out to share that the Course has a lot to offer, but they are not as valuable to your pursuit as the original.

Please do not be concerned about the page count in the volume mentioned as there are three separate processes included.

The Core message is straightforward:

> "Nothing real can be threatened.
> Nothing unreal exists.
> Herein lies the peace of God."

6 - Study and Prayer Are Perfect Together

Each of us can find difficulty in understanding what is going on in our thinking. While the study is lovely, the material that one is taking in is being filtered through the understanding that may have helped the illusion be accepted even when it was less than optimal.

There are many groups throughout the world that study the course in a small meeting where everyone can have a chance to share. When a student shares, others can listen for continuity in order to help the sharer feel their opinions of the clarity that the listener can hear in words spoken.

If listeners can hear the one speaking being incongruent with the course material, then that can be pointed out so that the internal perspective can be sifted appropriately to fine tune the base of understanding going forward. The notice and sharing of incongruity shift the listener into a co-creative co-contributor to the miracle in the thought embryo.

Building your life is like making a house in that the foundation is very pivotal to the success of the structure. A group member can help others to develop their understandings in ways that are solid and efficient.

The additional benefit of groups is to help students of the course to edit ideas that could confuse them.

Groups could be looked for both online and in the neighborhoods of the cities.

7 - A Lesson A Day for A Year

The Course has 365 lessons and most years have the same number of days. It would be easy enough for you to select a lesson a day and just read and see what you can integrate.

Group energy can be very beneficial to enliven the experience for you.

If You Do Both, You Will Likely Find Some Congruencies That Could Be Remarkable.

One Lesson May Be Enough To Change Your Life Enough To Put Your Problems In Perspective Enough So You Can Find Your Personal Peace.

There Is No Rush

There Is No Stress

I Recommend The Course For Your Consideration

9 - The Course Can Change Your Ability to Serve & Support Others

The course can bring you to personal peace and the awareness of the power of your intention and your discernment.

When you change your mind, you can channel the power of your personal perspective differently. Your thoughts are your filters, and your emotions can amplify the effect of those thought filters and efficiently shift height and width of all that is caught in the screen and all that flows through.

Your understanding of the power of the free will that has been granted to you by the God Most High can be both gratifying and intimidating. While freedom is power and authority, it is also a responsibility that can be quite heavy if you lose sight of the support that can help you to serve and support others.

When you feel that you have found the purpose of your life, you may feel a heavy responsibility, or you can remember to ask for the support you need to complete an assignment. The course will help you see that everything can be much more straightforward than it might seem.

Invite your "I' to melt into the collective "We, " and you will quickly realize that much more is possible than you ever thought.

10 - Miracles Are Different For Everybody

Be not concerned with judging others or declaring what is right and wrong; your creator is the one in charge of all that. Be concerned with your guidance and your services so that you give God a reason to smile.

When you are listening to others, you have the opportunity to learn about how they process, and from them, you can learn more about how you do it. When you see where they have a chance to create an optional outcome, you can also see that you have options in your life.

Would you go back if you could and change some things? The truth is that the minute that you read this is the first minute of the rest of your life and you can make new choices that will take you to a new place in your future.

This may sound good but seem impossible to do. It is understandable if a piece of you will be whispering that it is impossible for you to have that much power. Fear not for you will have high energy when you claim it.

When you started to read this book, you may have expected Miracles of physical healing. I am always amazed at what comes into my awareness regarding the physical, emotional, mental and spiritual miracles.

You can also be amazed when you prepare to see the messages and miracles that are intended for you. I would love to read someday about all that you can invite.

When you embrace the course a bit, it can be compared to adding software to your hard drive, so you have more depth and functionality. As you continue to process the wisdom of the course, your software is finessed into higher functionality.

As you study and learn and grow, clarity of spiritual connectivity can also develop and surprise you as your understanding flows ever more freely. I encourage you to learn from the course about optimizing your ability to act according to the purpose of your Soul.

I share my observations and experiences. Yours will be different as are you.

11 - Space & Perspective

The course can help you find space that you need to be the person who you have been born to be so you can do the work of your Soul for the people of your God. The course can lead you through the illusion and the distractions to the pure essence of the alignment which can allow you to pivot between the physical and the non-physical worlds.

When you do the course, you will arrive at a new level of intensity and intention and awe. The vibration of all you see can permeate the space and leave it charged forever even if it is portable.

The perspective you can find through realigning your thinking to see through the eyes of love instead of the eyes of hate and fear can be breathtaking. When you catch your breath again, everything can be seen in a new way which allows much more peace in your life.

The newly found peace can be shared freely so that many others can benefit from your discovery. The world needs the order that you can bring and bringing it can be very satisfying.

When you are ready and peaceful, consider who in your world might be open to hearing about your newfound peacefulness which can balance the less than joyful events in their life.

12 - Sacred Space

As you invite miracles through the course, or blessing or prayer, you can change the resonance of the space within you and space you are in. As vibration is raised, the depth can infiltrate the area and leave a residual harmonic.

Just like your personal emotional experiences can raise or lower your level of joy, your conscious triggering of how you choose to feel can do the same. Like an exercise that you frequently do which gets easier, conscious emotional triggering can bring ease for you in selecting the level of joy you wish to see

The changes in you and your space allow you to trigger your location in this or that world quickly. This is a tremendous place of empowerment for yourself.

Careful and respectful use of this gift can efficiently amplify your ability to serve numerically and geographically.

I invite you to be diligent and methodical in your use of new awareness that comes when you are a blessing or blessed by/with the vibration resonating.

Space can permeate you to the degree that it can be there when you intend that it be on demand. Listen but do not be surprised when you are used as a messenger of vocal miracles.

Your world will be different when you study, embrace, see, hear, feel, invite and share miracles and today that can be real.

13 - Helping Yourself and Others

The Course Can Help You Understand You

&

You Can Help Others
To Understand Themselves

&

You All Can Learn About Spiritual
Connectivity

Mike

You Request

Via Faith

&

God Delivers

15 - The Wrap-up

Your arrival on planet earth was by Divine Design, and the mission of your soul is most sacred. This planet is full of all kinds of distractions, and it is difficult for all of us to make our own decisions when we hear conflicting things from sources who represent authority

It is not easy being you and it is not easy for anyone else to be who they have been sent here to be. Once you acknowledge that we are all struggling, it becomes easier to realize that struggle exists to help us build spiritual muscle.

Every day we change ever so slightly that we cannot see it happening. We can expand our awareness of the human experience, and that can help.

If we were to be always alone, there would not be as many people around for us to talk. If you haven't noticed, many people speak but say little of value.

When you work A Course In Miracles, you can learn to see what is to be seen, to hear what is to be understood and discern about it all.

You have been invited to own your significance. The course can help. You can always choose how you interpret what you find.

16 - When You See Miracles

When you see a miracle manifest, please consider sharing it if you can do it while maintaining the privacy of the receiver. The stories about miracles can help people learn about the love of creator that can empower lives.

The world that we live in has a huge number of distractions. It can be difficult for some people to know for sure about the value of spiritual connectivity.

Real stories about healing can be heard and felt and then owned, and that can change a life.

You can release the stories online or in your own books or e-books or audio books or on YouTube.com as you see fit. If you would like me to consider publishing any, just send me an e-mail with your intentions.

I will not be able to use everything that is sent, but I will consider it if it might be aligned with my future projects.

For

Considering

These

Ideas

Ever

It Does Not Help Prayer Still Does!

Resource: http://www.Create-A-Prayer.com

19 - Resource Books

Distant Healing Sessions (or Join Mail List) – Write To mikewann@voicenet.com

Books by Rev. Mike at **www.Amazon.com**

Veterans Healing Six Pack
1. *Trauma Healing Options for VA Hospitals: Help for Veterans to Own Their Healing and their future.*
2. *Trauma Healing Action Steps for Veterans: Help to Start Healing*
3. *Trauma Healing Action Steps for Veterans: Empowerment*
4. *Trauma Healing Action Steps for Veterans: Forgiveness*
5. *Trauma Healing Action Steps for Veterans: Thought Freedom*
6. *Tea For Veterans: Welcome One Home*

PTSD Power Pack:
1. *The PTSD Project: Turn Pain To Power*
2. *PTSD & Soul Retrieval: Putting One Back Together*
3. *PTSD & The Purple PAD: Calling all Scientists and PTSD Patients*

Angel Raphael Speaks Volume 1: Take Courage! God Has Healing in Store for You!
Angel Raphael Speaks Volume 2: Take Courage! God Has Healing in Store for You!
Angel Raphael Speaks Volume 3: Take Courage! God Has Healing in Store for You!
Angel Raphael Speaks Volume 4: Angels, Addicts, Alcoholics & Prisoners – Oh Yeah!
Angel Raphael Speaks Volume 5: Prisoners Caring for Alcoholics - Australia In Miniature Projects Intro
Angel Raphael Speaks Volume 6: Prisoners Caring for Addicts - Australia In Miniature For Addicts
Reiki Journaling from Japan
Reiki Is Alive: God's Great Gift
Four Parts to Healing
Distant Healing: We Are All Connected
Stress Release Energy Work: How To Cope
Does Reiki Love Heal Cancer?
Group Consciousness
Salute To Philadelphia VA Medical Center: Thank You
Reiki Transcript for Reiki 2 & 3 Channels: Dr. Usui Is That You?
God Bless Kindle & Amazon
Puppies Are Different From People
If Your Dog Dies
Toy Guns Are Obsolete
Great Spirit Made Children With Red Skin: AND

The Cage of Fear: Is Not Locked
God Made Children Red, Yellow, Brown, Black & White: Greet Each Child...
Emergency Medical Kindness In The Cradle Of Liberty: Big City - Cracked Bell
Angels Are Always Around Addicts and Addicts: Help Is Near Now! Invite It In!
Angels Are Always Around Addicts and Alcoholics: Volume 2 - Tools To Help Re-Light...
Prison Jobs Now: Providing Care For Addicts And Addicts
Controlled Care Communities Concept
Prison Possibilities Dialogue Series: Concept
Prison Possibilities Dialogue Series: Volume 2, 3, 4, 5 Dialogues
Prison Possibilities Voluntary Exile
Prison Possibilities Corrections Coaches
Prison Possibilities For Mexicans: Is A Boat Better Than A Wall?
Prison Possibilities Family Time: A Reason to Thrive!
Prison Genius Pool: "So Much Genius In Jail."
Prison Possibilities Access Control: Prisoner Access by Request
Prisoner's Lawyers Can Save The American Economy: Make A Buck Doing It & ...
Prisoner Family Talks, Days, Stays & Vacations: Connecting Helps Healing
Prisoner Writing Projects: Write To Heal, Start Over & Reconnect
Prison Cell Clearing & Blessing: Clear Entities, Chase Ghosts, & Create Sacred Space
Prisoner Professors: Show You Are Aware Create Change With Care
Prison Reiki? Maybe Someday? A Gateway To Help Heal Prisons & America?
Judges and An Angel Rule On Possibilities: We Can Cut Sentences & Prison Costs
Ideas For Prison Wardens: Leadership Is Not Easy
Solitary Community: Could Community Support Cut Costs and Issues?
Prison Project Communications Team: Communications Can Change Lives
Motivating & Empowering Prisoners? Invite Prisoners To Find Their Motivation
Prison Segmentation For Safety, And Sanity, Security, Peace, and Space
Prison Segmentation For Security
Dowsing for Prisoners; Answers from Above
Ex-Prisoner Possibilities With Real Estate Investors
Prison Segmentation For Joint Ventures
Prison Segmentation For Your Rehabilitation: R U Ready?
Prison Segmentation For Family Villages
Prison Segmentation For Senior Prisoners
Prison Segmentation For Coaching Clubs

Little Books at Kindle.com by Rev. Mike:
English Medical History Questionnaire For Non-English Speakers
English Language Helper For Non-English Speakers
Wise Wonderful Women Are The Well Of The Family
Answers for Test & Research: Dowsing Power
Crisis? Reiki! Baby? Reiki!   Bible References For Healing
Angel Raphael Speaks – Prisons   Angel Raphael Speaks – Veterans
The Saint Off Interstate 95

20 - Angels Please Prayers

Addict's

Angels of Healing Selected
Help Me to Stay Directed
Come To Me From The Sky
I Am Ready to Succeed Not Try
If I Don't Invite You In
I Might Not Win
I Have Been Lost For Too Long
Help Me To Stay Strong

Alcoholic's

Angels of Healing On High
Help Me to Stay Dry
Come To Me From The Sky
I Am Ready to Succeed Not Try
If I Don't Invite You In
I Might Not Win
I Have Been Lost For Too Long
Help Me To Stay Strong

From

http://AngelRaphaelSpeaks.com/AAAAAAA/

21 - Private Channeling

Angel Raphael Speaks a series of free messages that are channeled through Reverend Mike Wanner for the Highest good and Highest Healing of all concerned.

Many questions arise about Reverend Mike doing private channeling, and he does help with that so e-mail him.

Reverend Mike is available worldwide as a psychic channel, emotional release facilitator, spiritual energy practitioner & teacher, and public speaker. He looks forward to meeting you soon!

Email - mikewann@voicenet.com 215-342-1270 PRIVATE SPIRITUAL READINGS/channelings or Spiritual Healing Sessions: Telephone or in person. Rev. Mike is available for private, one-on-one intuitive sessions with you, his Guide Family, and your Guides. He helps by offering clarity on emotional situations about your life, your purpose, your spirituality, and the release of stuffed emotions and cellular memory.
Connect to the love of your Guides today!
Contact Rev. Mike for an appointment.

Sessions available:

Spiritual Readings
Angel Channeling
Distant Reiki Healing
Remote Clearing of Stuffed Emotions
Distant Clearing Cellular Memory
Distant Clearing Energy Blockages
Remote Clearing of the Chakras
Customized needs
Mastermind dowsing responses to yes/no direction finding questions.

Rev. Mike is a facilitator of healing. He brings you and the Divine together so that you can align with the Divine and have a great time and a great life. All healing is between you and God, as it should be. Go ahead and start without Rev. Mike. Visit his prayer site http://www.Create-A-Prayer.com. Take the first step NOW.

22 - Reverend Mike Wanner

Rev. Mike Wanner started his Metaphysical and Ministerial studies with Reiki in 1993 and had studied seven styles of Reiki in the U.S., Japan, Canada, Denmark and Australia. He is certified to teach. He became certified to teach Integrated Energy Therapy in 1999 and co-taught the first IET class of the new Millennium. Mike began dowsing in 2001.

Ordained as a Metaphysical Minister of the International Metaphysical Ministry and an Interfaith Minister of the Circle of Miracles Ministry, Rev. Mike practices and teaches spiritual energy therapies in the Philadelphia Area.

Rev. Mike holds ministerial degrees from the University of Metaphysics and the University of Sedona. He is a Pastoral Care Associate at Aria - Frankford Hospital. He taught at the National Academy of Massage Therapy and Health Sciences.

Rev. Mike was a faculty member of the Medical Mission Sister's Center for Human Integration's School of Integrated Body/Mind Therapies in Fox Chase, Philadelphia, PA for twelve years.

Rev. Mike is licensed by the teaching of Intuitional Metaphysics to practice Spiritual Healing and Scientific Prayer. Mike is also a Prayer therapist.

Rev. Mike was elected in 2007 to the status of "Fellow of the American Institute of Stress."

In 2008, Rev. Mike became a practitioner of Coincidental Recognition as he incorporated the CoRe System into his spiritual healing practice.

In 2009, Rev. Mike trademarked a new healing process called Quantum Quatro! Subtle Energy System Support®.

In 2011, Rev. Mike joined the outreach program known as the Health Advantage Group.

In 2012, Rev. Mike became a Certified Professional Coach by The Master Coaching Academy and Joined the Personal Empowerment Group.

Before his Metaphysical, Ministerial and Coaching studies, Rev. Mike worked for Sears Roebuck and Co. while in High School and after graduation, until he joined the U. S. Air Force in 1965. He returned to Sears from Vietnam in 1969 and stayed until 1978. His final Sears assignment was as an efficiency expert in Methods - Operational Research and Development.

He volunteered with Burholme Emergency Medical Services from 1969 and is still a Life Member and Board of Directors Member. He started a private ambulance company in 1975 and worked professionally in the field until 2001 when he devoted his full attention to real estate investing, healing, coaching, and writing.

May All Who Read This Be Blessed
AND SO IT IS!

www.ingramcontent.com/pod-product-compliance
Lightning Source LLC
Chambersburg PA
CBHW030040230526
45472CB00002B/605